FASHION INDEPENDENT

The Original Style of Ann Bonfoey Taylor

FASHION INDEPENDENT
The Original Style of Ann Bonfoey Taylor

EDITED BY DENNITA SEWELL

PHOENIX ART MUSEUM

Fashion Independent: The Original Style of Ann Bonfoey Taylor was published in conjunction with an exhibition of the same title organized by and presented at Phoenix Art Museum from February 27 to May 29, 2011.

First edition
Printed in the United States of America

ISBN: 978-0-9844081-1-5

Published by
Phoenix Art Museum
1625 North Central Avenue
Phoenix, Arizona 85004
www.phxart.org

Distributed by
D.A.P./Distributed Art Publishers, Inc.
155 Sixth Avenue
2nd Floor
New York, New York 10013
Tel: 212-627-1999
Fax: 212-627-9484
www.artbook.com

Editor and Exhibition Curator: Dennita Sewell
Curatorial Assistant: Helen Nosova
Design: Chaves Design
Copyeditor: Elizabeth Stepina Zinn

Printed by O'Neil Printing, Phoenix, Arizona
Binding by Roswell Book Binding, Phoenix, Arizona

Front jacket: Cristóbal Balenciaga, Evening dress and coat, 1962–63 (detail). Abraham silk. See page 97.
Photograph by Ken Howie.
Frontispiece: Ann Bonfoey Taylor, 1971. Photograph by Toni Frissell.
Colophon: Ann Bonfoey Taylor, 1967. Photograph by Toni Frissell.
Back jacket: Ann Bonfoey Taylor, c. 1967. Photograph by Toni Frissell.

CONTENTS

EXHIBITION AND CATALOGUE SPONSORS

PRESENTING SPONSOR
U.S. Trust

SUPPORT FOR THE CATALOGUE PROVIDED BY
Barbara Anderson Stoiber

MAJOR SUPPORT PROVIDED BY
The Ruth and Vernon Taylor Foundation
The Virginia M. Ullman Foundation

ADDITIONAL MAJOR SUPPORT PROVIDED BY
Arizona Costume Institute
Barbara and Craig Barrett
Jacquie Dorrance
The Bruce T. Halle Family Foundation
Ellen Katz
Sharron Lewis
Miriam and Yefim Sukhman

SUPPORTING SPONSORS
Susan Drescher-Mulzet
Gay Wray

FOREWORD

For over four decades, Phoenix Art Museum has been devoted to building a high-quality collection of American and European fashion design, one of our seven curatorial areas of focus. The Museum has also presented numerous important, nationally recognized exhibitions, most recently under the imaginative eye of Dennita Sewell, Curator of Fashion Design. *Fashion Independent: The Original Style of Ann Bonfoey Taylor* is that rare moment when collection, exhibition, and curator come together to create a greater whole. Ann Bonfoey Taylor led an exciting, experiential life from her earliest days until her death in 2007. Her adventuresome way of living and noteworthy style, often featured in the country's leading lifestyle magazines, made her a model for the modern American woman. In her younger years, she created popular skiwear designs, and, in the postwar era, she began collecting and wearing the finest designs by the very best international designers, including Balenciaga, Fortuny, Givenchy, Madame Grès, and Charles James. In 2008 Vernon Taylor, Jr., and family generously gifted her outstanding wardrobe to Phoenix Art Museum.

The presentation of *Fashion Independent: The Original Style of Ann Bonfoey Taylor* is a great achievement for Phoenix Art Museum. The Museum began collecting American and European fashion design in the late 1960s, when the Arizona Costume Institute formed a support group for fashion design. Today the collection comprises over six thousand pieces ranging in date from the late seventeenth century, when few designers were recognized, to the present day, when figures such as Jean-Paul Gaultier and Ralph Rucci have achieved celebrity status. The study of fashion provides an understanding of eras in all cultures, and this exhibition highlights both the golden age of Parisian couture as well as the development of functional sportswear in mid-century America, the unique combination of which formed the core of Taylor's original style. Taylor had the ability to recognize great designers, the eye to acquire their most iconic works, and the flair to utilize her own creativity in wearing them. The Taylor family, in selecting Phoenix Art Museum as the repository of her wardrobe, honors our institution for the years of effort in collecting, presenting, and publishing the world's greatest fashion. It is a gift such as this, and the exhibition it has inspired, that maintains our fashion design collection's reputation as one of the finest in the country.

James K. Ballinger
SYBIL HARRINGTON DIRECTOR

If I had to describe Mrs. Ann Bonfoey Taylor, I would speak first of her great personality, very classic beauty, and impeccable style. It was an honor to dress her, and I immensely enjoyed advising her in the choice of her clothes.

She knew perfectly what suited her and was able to adapt pieces, with a sense of rigor, to her personal style. She was so chic and could wear anything, yet she was intransigent in her great style and never gravitated to something that did not look like her.

For me she was a friend and the ideal customer to dress—her kindness and friendship were more than warm.

One also cannot be indifferent to the beauty of the Taylors as a couple. Tall, athletic, and full of distinction, they made the most surprising and spectacular pair.

—HUBERT DE GIVENCHY

Ann Bonfoey Taylor wearing a Givenchy coat, 1960s.

INTRODUCTION

Original, bold, athletic, and gracious, Ann Bonfoey Taylor created a life that personifies a dream of what an American woman can be. Described by friends and family as beautiful, fashionable, intelligent, fun, and a marvelous hostess, Taylor entertained friends and international dignitaries with her husband, Vernon Taylor, Jr., at their homes in Denver, Vail, and Montana, as well as in New York and abroad. Yet her accomplishments went far beyond being a renowned hostess; Taylor was also an Olympic skier, a championship tennis player, a licensed pilot and instructor during World War II, a successful skiwear designer, and a skilled sportswoman who mastered fox hunting, horse jumping, and shooting. Of her many talents, fashion was her greatest passion, and throughout her life she demonstrated exceptional judgment about clothes and style.

Selected as one of *Harper's Bazaar*'s One Hundred Great Beauties of the World in 1967 and featured in the pages of magazines such as *Harper's Bazaar, Town and Country*, and *Vogue* in over nineteen editorials from the 1930s to the 1970s, Taylor posed for prominent photographers such as Slim Aarons, Louise Dahl-Wolfe, Toni Frissell, Bob Richardson, and Edward Steichen. In the 1940s, her skiwear designs under the label Ann Cooke were featured in top fashion magazines and in the windows of Lord and Taylor and Bonwit Teller. In the postwar era through the 1970s, she assembled a couture wardrobe by the most gifted designers working at the time, including Balenciaga, Fortuny, James Galanos, Madame Grès, Givenchy, and Charles James, along with custom-designed sportswear tailored to her specifications for every activity she participated in. Taylor's style was classic and sophisticated but had great flair. Equally adept at both vigorous outdoor pastimes and more refined, elegant entertainments, she brought her discerning eye for fashion to all pursuits. This truly unique ability made her an established tastemaker who deserves reconsideration as a style icon today.

In 2008 Vernon Taylor, Jr., and family donated Ann Bonfoey Taylor's extraordinary wardrobe to Phoenix Art Museum's celebrated fashion design collection. The gift is one of the most spectacular and prestigious donations in the Museum's fifty-year history, and it was selected by *Art and Antiques* magazine as one of the top one hundred museum gifts of 2008. Taylor's collection is significant in both the quality of the works and also in the magnitude and completeness of the wardrobe. It comprises masterful garments by the aforementioned

Ann Cooke, *Vogue*, August 1, 1933.
Photograph by Edward Steichen.

designers and includes rare and important examples of couture daywear, such as wool coats by Charles James and matching double-faced wool suit and dress ensembles by Madame Grès, which lend new insight into their designs. The collection also features Taylor's custom-designed bespoke riding, shooting, and sporting attire. Over time these works will serve as keystones in many exhibitions and will undoubtedly be appreciated by generations to come.

Taylor did not know her clothes were going to a museum. She saved them because she loved them and had a deep appreciation of every aspect of their design and construction. It is quite remarkable, then, that when selecting works for the museum's collection very little editing needed to be done. The simple reason is that her personal wardrobe was well edited in the first place. Each piece was carefully considered and intended for long-term use; no garment revealed itself as a spontaneous or odd purchase. Cohesive in style and color, the majority of the clothes feature minimalistic designs in a palette of neutral grays and blacks, accented by jewel tones for evening. Design characteristics such as sleeves on evening gowns, waistlines lowered in the back, and solid, textured fabrics are some of the common themes that repeat among the garments. Taylor knew with assurance what colors she looked best in, what shapes flattered her figure, and what designs would portray her as classic yet individual and stylish. Hubert de Givenchy echoed this sentiment in his tribute to Taylor in this catalogue, remarking that she "was intransigent in her great style and never gravitated to something that did not look like her."[1]

How did Ann Bonfoey Taylor develop her remarkable style? Curious, thoughtful, and observant, she had a zest for life—coupled with an incredible sense of practicality—that permeated everything she did. In times of hardship she was tenacious and forward thinking, and she fearlessly met challenges and obstacles head-on with verve. Her extraordinary personal drive led her to become a woman of impressive character, and it was through her strong sense of self that her distinctive style emerged.

Ann Cooke, 1930s.

Born in 1910 in Ardmore, Pennsylvania, Ann Bonfoey was the youngest child and only daughter of Lawrence and Octavia Bonfoey. Soon after Ann was born, the family moved to Quincy, Illinois, a small town on the banks of the Mississippi River, where Ann's maternal grandfather, E. N. Monroe, ran the Monroe Chemical Company, manufacturers of Putnam Dyes. In addition to working for the family business, Ann's father was an early aviation enthusiast and owned a little airport, Monroe Field, in a cornfield outside of Quincy. When Ann was six, her father first introduced her to flying in an open two-seater bi-plane, and, when she was twelve, he hired an instructor to teach her how to fly. Taylor explained in her autobiography, *Cleared for Take-Off*, "Our pilot wasn't a bit happy about this idea: back then nobody wanted to see a woman—let alone a young girl—fly a plane. But he had no choice."[2] For the next few years, Ann became quite accustomed to life around planes, and she often spent time in the sky with her three brothers, flying their father's Bellanca plane around the area.

As a teenager, Ann was sent to Briarcliff Manor, a fashionable boarding school in New York's Westchester County. A happy student, she was a member of the hockey, basketball, baseball, and swim teams, and she was also part of the athletic, riding, and music clubs. When she turned eighteen, her father encouraged her marriage to James Cooke, a freshman at Princeton University. Reluctantly, Ann agreed and the couple quickly had two children, Diane and Jay, before eventually settling in Burlington, Vermont. Newly thrown into the role of wife and mother, Ann embraced family life but also strove to maintain a sense of personal fulfillment outside the home. In the early-to-mid-1930s, she registered with the Models Guild in New York City. She posed for illustrations and ads for companies such as Colgate, Royal baking powder, Lux soap, and Lucky Strike cigarettes that ran in national magazines.

It was around the same time—prompted by the 1932 Winter Olympics in Lake Placid, New York—that skiing gained popularity in America. After moving to Burlington, Ann decided to take up the sport at the nearby village of Stowe. She spent many afternoons there learning how to ski, often climbing on her skis up a trail known as Nose Dive, returning home each night to care for her family. Several years later it was announced that the American women's Olympic ski squad was coming to Stowe to compete in a national race on Nose Dive, due to its many turns and difficulty. Ann's instructor encouraged her to participate in the race, and she ended up finishing in ninth place after falling near the end of the course and crawling over the finish line. Her performance and determination attracted the attention of the American officials, who invited her to train with the team for the 1940 Winter Olympics in Europe. Her daily training climbs on the slopes of Stowe also earned her the nickname Nose Dive Annie, which stuck with her for the rest of her life.

LOUISE DAHL-WOLFE

"Nose Dive Annie"

● Mrs. James Negley Cooke, Jr., has become so closely identified with Mt. Mansfield's crack ski trail that everyone calls her "Nose Dive Annie." She practically lives on it, and is so expert on its dizzy twists and schusses that when she enters a Nose Dive race the other entries blanch. This winter Mrs. Cooke, with her two children, has rented a made-over barn at Stowe, Vermont. Mr. Cooke, a top skier too, flies on for week-ends from their farm near Cleveland.

86

Opposite:
Ann Cooke ski racing while wearing her signature fanny pouch, 1930s.

Ann's U.S. National Ski Championship competitor's bib, 1939. Collection of New England Ski Museum.

Above:
Ann Cooke, *Harper's Bazaar*, March 1, 1941.

ANN SIMPKINS

• Ann Cooke describes herself as a "flying schoolmarm." She is, but her little red school-house is the Burlington Airport in Vermont, her scholars Army air cadets. She is one of twenty-five women in this country to hold an instructor's rating, one of a still fewer number instructing U. S. Army fliers. Instructress Cooke had her first fling at the air when she was six. Her father took her up in his open two-seater—she learned to pilot herself on the family airfield leveled in the corn at Quincy, Illinois, her home town. She married at nineteen, had two children, settled in Vermont, gave up flying for skiing. They called her Nose Dive Annie on the Mt. Mansfield slopes, she made the Olympic team, she had all the other skiers beaten hands down for looks. Two years ago as war loomed over the horizon, she went back again to flying, boned up in navigation like a nailer, within a year and a half earned her commercial license, instructor's rating, her present job at the Burlington Airport. Every morning, she gets into her ski pants and fur-lined hood; puts in an eight-hour day six days a week. The men have taken kindly to their dazzling teacher. When occasionally she gets an overly cocky student, she gives him a dose of air acrobatics —tortures which she itemizes casually as wringing out, spins, snap rolls, and chandelles.

ANN COOKE Instructor of Army Air Cadets

Opposite:

Harper's Bazaar, February 1943.

Left:

Ann Cooke, Burlington,

Vermont, 1943.

The next winter, Ann set off with her teammates to train in Sun Valley, Idaho, unbeknownst of two major events that were about to change her life. Later that season, her marriage to James Cooke ended after he left her for a fellow member of the ski squad. In a second blow, the Olympics were canceled due to the outbreak of World War II. Hurt and with no emotional or financial support from her ex-husband or family, Ann began to look around and think of how to pull herself up and care for her family.

Turning to aviation as the only thing she knew from her background to make money (as she later said, "I had to survive, I had no choice"), Ann enrolled at the University of Vermont and studied subjects related to flying. She also began to take flight lessons at the Burlington Airport. In the airport's all-male environment, it was a struggle for Ann to be taken seriously, but she persisted in her studies and patiently waited for one of the instructors to take her up in the air. After the bombing of Pearl Harbor in 1941, there was a new sense of urgency at the airfield. Taken under the wings of the chief pilot, Ann was put on the fast track to becoming a flight instructor. Soon after, she was tested by an Air Force examiner, awarded her commercial rating, made a C.A.A. War Training Service Instructor, and given her first five students—all in the same afternoon. Still gaining confidence in her own skills, Ann had to summon up great courage to take those first students up that day.

As a base-level instructor, Ann had only thirty-five hours of flying time to train the cadets before they were ready to enter combat. It was the first time many of the young men had been away from home, and they were homesick and insecure. Having a woman as an instructor, especially one as beautiful as Ann, was not what some of the cadets were expecting. Facing these men and the extreme challenges of the training conditions forced her to be tough and demanding, yet compassionate.

Later in life Ann spoke about this time with mixed feelings. On one hand, she was frustrated that she did not have the time to properly prepare the men; on the other hand, she was tremendously proud to serve her country. As a divorced woman with two children to support (at a time when that still held great stigma), Ann was most proud of her ability to make a life for herself and her children. Throughout the war years, she rose early, drove more than forty-five minutes to the airbase, trained her students, and returned home at night to have supper and care for her family. It was during this formative time that—like so many others who had been directly affected by the war—Ann developed the determination and drive that would define her character for the rest of her life.

Ann Cooke ski clothes advertisement.

Ann Cooke skiwear design featured on the cover
of *Harper's Bazaar*, January 1946.

After the war ended in 1945, many qualified pilots returned home to look for new jobs and Ann knew that, as much as she wanted to continue flying, she had a slim chance of getting work. One night at a cocktail party in Stowe, she accidentally stumbled into her next career—fashion. She had always designed her own ski clothes (including the first "fanny pack," which she used to carry lipstick and other amenities when she climbed) and that night many of the guests complimented what she was wearing. Ann offered, "If you want to come round for a drink tomorrow, I may have a few things I can sell."[3] The next day she sold everything, so she had a local seamstress make more and took them down to the *Harper's Bazaar* offices in New York, where she showed them to her friend and fashion editor Diana Vreeland. The magazine's editor-in-chief, Carmel Snow, granted Vreeland's request to feature the clothes in an editorial photographed on top of Mount Washington. Soon after, in January 1946, Ann's designs were again featured in the magazine, this time on the front cover with a six-page story inside:

> *Everything about this sweater is enormous—the bulk, the roundness, the chic. Made with great knowledge of wool, weather, and woman, it is hand-knit of heavy, deliciously spongy, springy wool which retains some of the natural oils that make sheep almost waterproof. The Forstmann woolen ski pants stretch long and lean, fitted to perfection. Both pieces (and even the sheep themselves) are from Vermont. The sweater, made to order, $35. The pants $38.50. Ann Cooke, Stowe, Vermont.*[4]

These articles launched a huge demand for her designs and so many orders began flooding in that Ann did not have the production facilities to fill them. At the time, her shop was in her house in Stowe. Her knitters were local farmers' wives and the yarn was unscoured Vermont wool colored with homemade dyes in one of the farm kitchens. Lord and Taylor arranged for increased production and gained exclusive distribution of Ann's designs, which they featured in the windows of their Fifth Avenue store. For Ann it was a moment of great success: "All of the hard work I have done picking myself up and here I am—I have done it." She was extremely proud of her perseverance and ability to support her children, proclaiming, "I did whatever I could to make a name for myself

Ann Cooke skiwear designs at Lord and Taylor, 1946.

Opposite: Models wearing Ann Cooke skiwear.

Above: Ann Cooke wearing her own design, photographed
on Mount Washington for "The Great White Way,"
Harper's Bazaar, January 1946.

and a life for myself. First in aviation and then in fashion."[5] Fashion became a source of empowerment for Ann, as it provided both a way to lift her family out of hard times and a way for her to develop something of her own. At a time when her fashion sense was beginning to solidify, it was incredibly liberating for Ann to achieve success through her designs.

Shortly thereafter, Ann met Vernon "Moose" Taylor, Jr., when he stopped into her shop to buy a pair of ski trousers on his way to Mont-Tremblant Ski Resort in Canada. Their chemistry was instant, and Ann took one look at him and decided he was for her. After Moose left the shop, Ann immediately invited a girlfriend to join her in Mont-Tremblant that weekend, feigning great surprise when they accidentally bumped into him while there. In the meantime, the zipper on the trousers he bought from her had broken. "Those ski clothes of yours . . . are the most appalling clothes I ever bought in my life!" he exclaimed.[6] She offered to buy him a drink later as an apology, and their romance began. Within two weeks (an eternity, in Ann's mind) they were engaged, and they married on May 21, 1946, in Greenwich, Connecticut (home of Julius Forstmann, owner of Forstmann wool). Ann's hometown newspaper ran a wedding announcement several days later:

> *Charming Mrs. Taylor chose a light grey suit for her marriage and wore a green band in her hair. She carried a cabbage rose, the newest in bridal bouquets, designed of petals of dozens and dozens of roses into one large blossom. Her bouquet was fashioned of Briarcliff roses.*[7]

For the first three years of their marriage, the couple was based in Texas, as Moose followed in his father's footsteps in the oil business. Soon after their wedding, Ann had a whirlwind tour back to New York to take care of her business and design costumes for the Radio City Music Hall Christmas Production. All the attention and press she was receiving for her fashions was very glamorous, but she knew her design career was limited and would not bring her long-term happiness. One evening in New York, she received a Western Union telegram from Moose that read, "Take off your golden slippers, woman. Come home to hard reality."[8] So she decided to retire from the fashion business and returned to Texas to join Moose. This marked the beginning of their very happy marriage and family life.

Opposite: Mr. and Mrs. Vernon Taylor, Jr., married May 21, 1946.

Left and above: The Taylors skiing at Sun Valley and on their honeymoon in Bermuda.

In 1951 the Taylors moved to Denver, Colorado, and would eventually establish a family of four boys—Vernon, Douglas, Robert, and Craig—in addition to Ann's children from her first marriage. Although Ann loved New York and would have preferred to live there, she adored Moose and was happy to make her life with him out west. As she had in Vermont, she took up and perfected the regional sporting activities, including hunting for coyotes on horses, horse jumping, and shooting. She had a wonderful new life but also faced many challenges. Moose's parents had not approved of the union. At the time, it was still quite a social scandal for a divorced mother of two to remarry. Yet Ann was secure in both herself and her marriage, and, as she had many times before, she set judgment aside and focused on being an accomplished woman and supportive wife in every way possible.

The Taylors quickly became known for their hospitality and legendary entertaining. Ann was involved in every aspect of the home and took great care to ensure that every last detail was executed to perfection following proper etiquette. Beyond aesthetic appearances, it was also very important to Ann to be well informed, bright, and articulate. She read voraciously daily. Before an event, she would read a book about her guests' interests so she could engage in intelligent conversation with them. Her son Robert remembers how she thumbed through a book and picked various passages to learn about a subject. Books filled every room of the home—all types of books but especially those on history and personalities. *The British Stable* by Giles Worsley, *Vanishing Africa* by Leni Riefenstahl, *The Private World of the Duke and Duchess of Windsor* by Hugo Vickers, *Madame de Pompadour* by Colin Jones, and *Clothes and Horse: A Guide to Correct Dress for All Riding Occasions* by Sydney D. Barney are just a sampling of the thousands of titles.

On the day of a big party, Ann was up at five in the morning helping with the flowers and all the other arrangements: "She worked just as hard as anyone else," her youngest son, Craig, remembers. "She appreciated the same qualities in other people and did not look approvingly to those who took things for granted and weren't making an effort."[9] Every afternoon from 4:30 to 5:00 Ann would prepare for the evening. This ritual included setting her hair, cleansing her face, applying cream, doing her make-up, and finally, her favorite part, putting together her ensemble. Methodical and steady, this was her time to situate herself. The extraordinary experience

Vernon Taylor, Jr., family home, Vail, Colorado.

of attending a dinner or event at the Taylor home began with a distinguished sense of arrival. Guests to the Denver house traveled down a long driveway flanked by a white fence before reaching the large circular drive in front of the 1930s stone residence. Ann was always ready and waiting to greet the guests between 6:00 and 6:30. Inside, all the elements were perfectly coordinated to create the most inviting environment—music played softly, fresh flowers were coordinated in each room, a fire burned at the perfect level, and spritzer was in the air. The entire scene created a welcoming sense of luxurious ease. The night continued with cocktails in the library at 6:30, followed by dinner at 7:30, and then after-dinner coffee and drinks in the library, which allowed for guests to mix and mingle, linger, or leave at their own discretion.

In 1963, the Taylors built one of the first residences in Vail, Colorado, and they also owned a working ranch in Montana. Moose was one of Vail's original investors, and the Taylors did much to help create the village, attracting important people and elevating its reputation as an elegant and glamorous ski destination. From its opening season in 1962, Vail was promoted with lavish articles in leading magazines, many through Ann's connections. The Taylors' spectacular French Manor style home set the benchmark for the resort's future, and it became their center of entertaining during the winter season. Some of the many distinguished guests from New York and abroad included the actors Cliff Robertson, Dina Merrill, and Charlton Heston; author Truman Capote; Mr. and Mrs. Henry Kissinger; Lewis Preston, President of J. P. Morgan; Mr. and Mrs. Thomas J. Watson, Chairman of IBM; Mr. and Mrs. Thomas Kempner, Chairman of Loeb Partners; and Gianni Agnelli, head of Fiat. Aided by Ann's signature attention to detail and gracious hosting, parties at the Taylor home mixed across generations well—something that is rare and hard to do. Thomas Kempner, Jr., recalled the experience of attending one of the Taylors' Vail parties as a teenager. He remembered how glamorously everyone was dressed—especially Mrs. Taylor, and it was always *Mrs.* Taylor—and was struck by how interested she was in her son's friends and felt she was really listening to what he had to say. She seemed bigger than life to him—even at her average 5'7" height.[10] Although the parties followed a formal schedule and standard of etiquette, they were fun and there was laughter all around the table. Ann was known for her wonderful wit and keen perception of people, along with her great memory. Every guest walked away feeling special.

The ski chateau that is Vail's contribution to the simple life of the snows finds perhaps its ultimate expression in the home of Mr. and Mrs. Vernon Taylor, Jr. Mrs. Taylor, poised here on a carved French bench with her ski boots uncompromisingly on the Chinese Aubusson, is one of Vail most energetic hostesses; she also designs her own ski clothes. Her husband is a stockholder in the Vail Corporation and an original partner; their home is in Denver, but every winter they move, staff and all, to Vail for the season.

"THE PERFECT MOUNTAIN," HOLIDAY, MARCH 1, 1964

The headdress is Arabian and designed for the desert but the lady inside is an American and she is wearing it on a ski slope. Mrs. Vernon Taylor of Denver is a dedicated skier and world traveler with an eye for improbable but practical ski clothes. She saw this headgear in Saudi Arabia and figured that since it has protected against the wind and blowing sand for centuries it would provide fine protection against wind and blowing snow. . . . Along with her Arab headdress she has items from Greece, England, Austria and France.

"AN INVENTIVE SKIER'S WORLDLY WARDROBE," LIFE, JANUARY 1965

In Greece, Mrs. Taylor found an Evzone costume worn by mountain troops. To wear with it she thought up racing-stripe stockings.

"AN INVENTIVE SKIER'S WORLDLY WARDROBE," LIFE, JANUARY 1965

A skiier of enormous dash, who thinks ski clothes should
have more of it—that's Mrs. Vernon Taylor, Jr. . . .
Wherever she goes, Mrs. Taylor keeps an eye out for
vervy bits of equipment to enliven her classic ski gear:
here, some recent acquisitions . . . . two swashbuckling
Scottish sporrans, a U.S. Civil War soldier's
cap (all from antique shops here or
abroad) . . .with fine impartiality,
Mrs. Taylor owns two Civil War
caps—blue and grey.

"THE GREAT SKI LIFE WIT AND
DASH ADDED BY MRS. VERNON
TAYLOR, JR.," VOGUE,
NOVEMBER 1, 1969

Mrs. Taylor's ideas are as practical as they are picturesque—
take the sporrans, for example. They're worn by Scotsmen as
purses, by Mrs. Taylor for exactly the same purpose—she tucks
money, lip gloss, ski-lift tickets into them. . . .Lately, she's
been on a military kick: recent hats include, beside the two
Civil War caps, a British hussar's plumed busby said to have
been worn at the Battle of Balaclava.

"THE GREAT SKI LIFE WIT AND DASH ADDED BY MRS.
VERNON TAYLOR, JR.," VOGUE, NOVEMBER 1, 1969

When asked why he had chosen Marisa Berenson to star in
Barry Lyndon, Stanley Kubrick, who directed the ponderous
epic, answered, "She wears hats so well!" The same can be said
of Mrs. Vernon Taylor from Denver, Colorado . . . She thinks as
she pleases, does as she likes and wears hats with even greater flair
than Marisa Berenson. Her husband is a real estate tycoon of the
first magnitude; while she is an original.

"THE 101 HATS OF MRS. VERNON TAYLOR,"
TOWN AND COUNTRY, MARCH 1977

Spending winters in Vail also gave Ann the opportunity to continue her love of skiing and ski fashion. In the 1960s, *Vogue*, *Harper's Bazaar*, *Town and Country*, *Holiday*, and *Life* ran numerous articles about Ann's original and bold ski attire. She favored sleek-fitting silhouettes in a mostly dark color palette, noting that all-black attire made one "stand out against the elements in strong positive shapes."[11] She also began to incorporate items she saw on her travels into her skiwear, including an Arabian headdress (to protect one's head from the snow, as featured in a full-page spread in *Life* magazine), a Grecian mountain troop uniform (paired with sleek, racing-stripe stockings), and other military-based fashions, such as a wide variety of hats and headpieces. These improbable, yet often practical, choices show Ann's resourcefulness and flair for the unique. They also established her as one of the most dashing sportswomen of her time.

In Montana, Ann enjoyed a combination of entertaining, riding, and flying over the wide-open countryside in gliders. Themes of red, white, and blue were predominant in their Victorian ranch style home, known as the Box Elder Ranch, and the Americana feel made it the perfect location for the Taylors' annual Fourth of July party. On the ranch, Ann adopted a practical wardrobe of formal riding clothes, or jeans and a white button-down shirt paired with a scarf, which allowed her to stay active. Indeed, whether she was in Denver, Vail, Montana, or abroad, Ann continued to practice the discipline of daily sport and exercise until the very end of her life—riding, playing tennis, and skiing well into her eighties.

Opposite: Ann Taylor, looking great in cowboy hat, Western shirt, and chaps—the standard equipment for an active day on Box Elder Ranch.
"Soaring in Montana," *Town and Country*, July 1974.

Above: Mr. and Mrs. Vernon Taylor, Jr., at Box Elder Ranch near Lewistown, Montana.

Taylor honed her inherent fashion sense the same way she became exceptional at everything else she did—through study, focus, and discipline. In the early 1950s, she began traveling to New York and later Paris to attend the fashion collection showings, meet with the top designers, and purchase couture clothing. Wearing couture was part of the social world she moved in with Moose, and the regimen of daily life required an appropriate wardrobe and several changes of clothes throughout the day.

The postwar era was the golden age of couture, when Paris regained its dominance and the entire direction of fashion was set by couture. Taylor chose to work with only a few of the very best designers, forming relationships with them rather than shopping broadly on the surface of many different houses. Her favorites—Balenciaga, Givenchy, Madame Grès, and Charles James—were all superb at cutting, and their work is characterized by a mastery of great restraint. Taylor's past experience as a successful designer aided her deep understanding and appreciation of every aspect of clothing design and construction. She knew what looked best on her slim, athletic frame, and she worked with the couturiers in dialogue to create clothes of excellent design personalized with individual touches made specifically for her.

In a recent interview, Moose remembered his wife's love of clothes: "She liked variations on a theme such as the many types of fox hunting and riding clothes. And, anything that was a little different. She always had her own ideas as to how she wanted them to look." Moose traveled with her to Paris and described a typical visit to Givenchy's studio: "We went up in a tiny little elevator—the two of us could hardly get in. The studio looked like a typical place where you would buy clothes with all sorts of needles and pins around. They would look at pictures of all kinds of clothes he had done and she would comment on them—things that she liked. She might see one costume but say she wished it had buttons going up the other side and comments like that." He recounted a similar selection process at Madame Grès, "Models would come in wearing the newest line of clothes and Ann would say, 'Well, I like that but the skirt should be longer,' and the next model would come out and she would say 'the sleeves should be shorter.'" Although Moose often accompanied her to designer's studios, he soon decided to reserve his comments on her choices: "I was to sit there while she tried on clothes and then she was to walk by me to see what I liked on her. Then she would say what she liked. We did that for awhile, then we got to the place where we weren't agreeing on anything that she liked or I liked on her. So, we decided to part ways on what her selection of clothes would be. And, we did!"[12]

Michelle Taylor similarly remembers her mother-in-law's discerning fashion sense: "She had an impeccable sense of proportion. She visually had an innate sense of what made her look best and what would be most flattering on a woman. She liked designers who appreciated the feminine form. She also had an acute appreciation of workmanship such as raglan sleeves and skirts cut on the bias. The clothes she wore were a mastery of proportion, design, and technique."[13] Taylor appreciated a garment not only for the way it looked but also for the way it functioned. The items she chose were extremely comfortable to wear—never too tight or fussy. Elaborate beading, embellishment, or flounces were unnecessary; a woman of Taylor's poise did not require bolstering by such ornamentation. Rather, her clothes possess an austere elegance that was highlighted to the best effect by her extraordinary carriage. Taylor spent a great deal of time selecting her fashions and attending fittings, and, ultimately, the time she spent ensured that she was purchasing clothes she could love and wear for a lifetime. Douglas Taylor remembers his mother's selectiveness: "Mother had a lot of clothes, but she was selective. She was frugal about things like that. She was never one to throw things away. She would keep them and use them repeatedly, not like women today who wear something once and then give it away. She would pay more for something that would last."[14] This mindset most certainly hearkens back to the struggles Taylor endured during the war, the impact of which stayed with her for the rest of her life.

Clothing was undoubtedly a great joy for Ann Bonfoey Taylor. Dressing correctly for each of the sporting activities she practiced on a daily basis and for dinner every evening was an integral part of the lifestyle she created for herself and her family. Ever appropriate, she possessed the extraordinary ability to look effortlessly chic in whatever she wore, yet she had a very distinct idea of how she wanted to present herself. Nancy Kissinger spoke poignantly of Taylor's signature style: "She was slim and athletic and was probably very easy to fit. She wore the clothes, they didn't wear her. She looked wonderful all the time and carried herself beautifully. She had a calm way of dressing. Very chic but not outlandish and it had an influence on people."[15] For Taylor, great style was not solely the product of great clothes; rather, it was a carefully crafted blend of fashion sense, intelligence, and poise. She leaves behind not only a terrific wardrobe of clothes but also a wealth of knowledge about the proper way a woman should dress and carry herself. Throughout her life, Taylor shared her opinions on fashion with those around her, both leading by example and instructing others, especially her family members, with direct criticism and compliments. Ashley Taylor recalled several principles her grandmother taught her:

> On Selecting Fashion
>
> Military always, but motorcycle never
> Polka dots and subtle prints are permissible, but never animal prints
> Long skirts at night
> Long dresses for black tie
> Cocktail attire is knee length
> Always maintain a feminine silhouette
> Big earrings
> Large cuff bracelets
> Always brooches
> Pink is good for nails, red is not
> Pink lipstick is good, red is not
> Your look isn't complete unless your hair is done[16]

These words of fashion wisdom are just a few of the guidelines Taylor followed, and, along with her extraordinary wardrobe, they encompass the core of what made her a creative and original fashion independent. Yet perhaps her more remarkable and lasting gift resides in the strength and spirit of character that defined her life. Taylor's eldest son, Vernon III, recognized his mother's resilient nature: "She was independent and had a strong sense of self. She was not going to allow herself to be put down by a bad marriage or the male-dominant culture of the day. She did exactly what she wanted and needed to do. That may not be a conventional definition of feminism, but she clearly was a woman ahead of her time. Through fashion and design, she discovered a way of expression that reflected her appreciation of beauty and style as well as who she was, both inside and out."[17] It was through this drive and determination that Ann Bonfoey Taylor became a true individual, one to whom the modern woman can look to for guidance in so much more than just style.

1. Hubert de Givenchy, see p. 9 of this volume.
2. Ann Taylor, *Cleared for Take-Off* (Classic Day Publishing, 1999), p. 3.
3. Ibid., pp. 38–39.
4. *Harper's Bazaar* (Jan. 1946), p. 71.
5. Ashley Taylor, interview with the author, June 2010.
6. Taylor (note 2), p. 40.
7. *Quincy Herald-Whig*, May 26, 1946, p. 4.
8. Taylor (note 2), p. 41.
9. Craig Taylor, interview with the author, April 2008.
10. Thomas Kempner, Jr., interview with the author, May 2010.
11. *Harper's Bazaar* (Dec. 1964), p. 128.
12. Vernon Taylor, Jr., interview with the author, Nov. 2010.
13. Michelle Taylor, telephone interview with the author, Dec. 2010.
14. Douglas Taylor, telephone interview with the author, Jan. 2011.
15. Nancy Kissinger, audio interview with David Boatman, Dec. 2010.
16. Ashley Taylor, interview with the author, Aug. 2010.
17. Vernon Taylor III, correspondence with the author, Dec. 2010.

550 PARK AVENUE

January 24, 1971

Dear Ann,

I have put off writing to you since our
meeting in my office first to have the
tape typed out and secondly, to really
think through your views and your
suggestions to us.

I do think this; I think that everything
you say is obviously true because you are
intelligent, you are interested, and this
is your reaction. The only thing we did
not get quite clear is whether it is you
who would like to know more about the
clothes, how to wear them, etc., or that
your heart bleeds for the women who do not
have your exposure such as going to France
-- being exposed to many people of different
nationalities and seeing the general picture
of clothes today.

Yes, it is true most women see very little
but as I repeat, I do not know why they are
so desperately interested. Somehow or
other, it must be in their bringing up that
though they desire everything, they have
never been trained to work that hard to
find out how to have what it is they most
want.

There is no question that dressing has a
great deal of education, sense of history
and economics and the social world within
it -- within the study of clothes. And if
people are going to be real perfectionists,
such as you are, it isn't that one has to be
rich, it is that one has to have an open
mind that is totally absorbed in today and
which never looks back.

Correspondence from Diana Vreeland, editor-in-chief of *Vogue*, to Ann Taylor, 1971.

I often feel that the average American woman has had one period in her life, perhaps when she was a young married woman, perhaps when she was a belle on the back porch at Memphis. And all her looks go back to that -- those were the days -- those were the clothes. They don't seem to want to run ahead of the pack, make mistakes, be idiotic, but enjoy themselves and feel that they really are getting the best out of the life that is there for them to have. I suppose that life is quite dull where there is no theatre and no great movement of different nationalities and perpetual change in entertainment. And that of course, you only get in three great cities in the world; London, Paris and New York.

However, I do not see why a woman living out of New York is not more satisfied with her lot as she obviously leads a healthy life. Every city today has museums, orchestras, visiting ballet, etc., etc. But somehow the American woman doesn't seem to educate herself, to keep up with the times which also, of course, include her clothes.

I know it maddens you for me to speak of youth, but it has always been my firm belief that fashion is only made for youth and everybody else has to compromise.

I am not speaking of what age *one is* I am talking about the bumps on your body, the length of your throat and the condition of your legs. One can be any age if one is, so to speak, a figure of youth -- all of which comes from a spirit and continual self education. *+ discipline*

Now I am writing all this to you, who unquestionably knows it all too well yourself, as you do dress so beautifully and have an extreme sense of fashion. It is going to be very hard indeed to tell an American woman to do something that she hasn't seen three other women do first. She never wants to be first. She always wants to be safe. Safe from what? Nobody knows. But safe.

Therefore, she criticizes and agonizes. The agony of not being on The Best Dressed List must be dreadful for them all. But they are not and its probably because they've never been seen and there is a public world of heroines who are admired for the way they turn themselves out -- but nobody is admired today unless they are creative and are capable of putting themselves together in a very personal way. *inventive -*

The today of the uniform good looks is behind us -- people who would like to wear the conservatism of the 50's should go right on doing it as they would probably look perfectly delightful as it would suit them and suite their dispositions as it is the way they want to look.

You were extremely nice to come in and be with us for about three-quarters of an hour and it was very interesting to hear your views.

I am keeping the tape and if you ever get an idea how -- what we could do to put over an angle to really help these women whom you claim need help -- we would be delighted to hear it from you.

You have always been marvelously generous with your time and we have called upon you for so very many things and all of us are deeply appreciative.

I hope you do not think I am too brutal, too thoughtless of people less fortunate than I have been -- and to have lived in so many countries and so many cities. And it is true I have been very fortunate but then, that is the life that I made for myself. I don't see why more women don't go out and do what they want to do if they think that that is the way, which it isn't necessarily for many people.

For instance, you yourself, Ann, have made a most marvelous life. I can remember years ago when you were in a marvelously creative mood which has never ceased and you just wanted everything and you just wanted everything to be right. Every place you've been you've made a great success of it.

When I saw you in Paris I thought you were the best turned out woman I'd seen for many years in Paris, as I don't feel that Parisiennes, with only a few exceptions, are so extraordinary.

This is a very very big subject we are discussing becuase it really all boils down to -- what do women want in life.

Of course they have to look after their teeth, their houses, their children and often on very very little money, their time taken with heavy work. This is unfortunate but true.

It seems to me curious that they are discontented as clothes today are so inexpensive and so glorious. We are specializing in them in Vogue, incidentally, and I think in each issue you will see how very inexpensive our clothes are.

Please let me know the next time you are in New York as it is always a joy to see you.

Again a million thanks for giving us that three-quarters of an hour.

Forgive this much to long letter —

affectionately

Diana —

Diana Vreeland

Opposite: Ann Bonfoey
Taylor, Long Island,
New York, 1971.

Above and left: The
Taylors on safari in
Kenya, 1965.

THE TAYLORS ABROAD

International travel was a large part of the Taylors' lifestyle. In their years together, they spent a lot of time abroad, and their trips to Europe and Africa especially influenced Taylor's legendary style. Always prepared and impeccably dressed for every situation, Taylor compiled a formidable arsenal of luggage to transport her wardrobe with the utmost care. The items featured on the following two pages represent her personalized collection of luggage that she traveled with all over the world.

  Former Ambassador of Ireland Walter Curley fondly recalls a memorable visit the Taylors made to Dublin: "I sent a car out to the airport to meet them and bring them in. The driver radioed me from the car, 'We are going to need another car for Mrs. Taylor's luggage.' So another car was dispatched just to bring the luggage and a guard with the luggage. When those two cars drove up the long drive to the embassy in Phoenix Park, the staff at the residence was amazed—their eyes jumped out of their heads. The guys carried up all those bags and the ladies had the time of their life unpacking Annie Taylor's fabulous clothes into the closets."

Ann Bonfoey Taylor's collection of personalized
LOUIS VUITTON, HERMÈS, and GUCCI luggage, 1960s–1970s

ANN BONFOEY TAYLOR AND TONI FRISSELL

Toni Frissell (1907–1988) had a distinguished and pioneering career specializing in fashion photography and informal portraiture. She first worked as a staff photographer for *Vogue*, later shot for *Harper's Bazaar* and *Sports Illustrated*, and was commissioned on several occasions by *Life*. In 1941 she volunteered her services to the American Red Cross and eventually became the official photographer of the Women's Army Corps, which led her to capture some of the most compelling images of World War II, including her often-published pictures of the Tuskegee Airmen. In 1970 Frissell donated her body of work, including a number of photographs of Ann Bonfoey Taylor, to the Library of Congress in Washington, D.C.

Frissell preferred active, athletic views of women, often posing models out of doors even when in evening dress. She first photographed Taylor as early as 1939 for a *Harper's Bazaar* profile of the Olympic ski squad, and, over the next three decades, she worked with Taylor on at least six articles published in *Town and Country*, *Vogue*, and *Life*. The two shared a love of fashion and held a mutual admiration for each other, becoming lifelong friends. "Toni liked mother's fashion sense and found her an easy person to work with," Douglas Taylor remembers. "Toni was easy to be around and chatty. She was always willing to do another shot and mother was always willing to try another pose. Mother put a lot of time and thought into the sessions. The ski sessions were especially challenging as they were taken in the late afternoon and it was freezing up in the mountains. It took the willingness of both the photographer and the model to get those shots." The photographs on these four pages were taken in 1971 at Frissell's estate in Long Island, New York.

She was a woman of taste who was also accomplished as a pilot, as a skier, as a Wimbledon tennis player, as a rider and shooter. There was a certain magic to her. And, one manifestation of it was her eye for fashion. She had many gifts but the one she was most proud of was having judgment about clothes and keeping together a collection of very remarkable designs by some of the best and most gifted fashion people, Balenciaga [and so on]. She had an appreciation of the clothes and understood how to put them together.

ROBIN CHANDLER DUKE

She was so chic. Women like this plotted my course in life. Diana Vreeland sent the editors and photographers out to shoot women like Mrs. Ann Bonfoey Taylor. I looked at them as a young person and I wondered why I was feeling a connection to this individual and then I slowly got it. I was plugged into her sparkling style—the way she did things, the way she entertained, the room. One aspect of her leads you to another. She had such an enormous influence on me from just one article in Vogue.

RALPH RUCCI

THE COLLECTION

Gift of Mr. Vernon Taylor, Jr., and family

In 2008 Vernon Taylor, Jr., and family donated Ann Bonfoey Taylor's extraordinary wardrobe of custom-made couture, sporting ensembles, and accessories to Phoenix Art Museum's celebrated fashion design collection. One of the most prestigious in the Museum's fifty-year history, the donation was selected by *Art and Antiques* magazine as one of the top one hundred museum gifts of 2008. Comprising two hundred pieces,

the collection includes sixty full ensembles and additional accessories catalogued under Museum accession numbers 2008.50–2008.200. Unless otherwise noted, all items in the following section are gift of Vernon Taylor, Jr., and family.

Detail of Henry Maxwell custom boot tree, late 1960s.

H. HUNTSMAN AND SONS

(English)
Riding jacket and vest, c. 1967
Wool

Breeches: HARRY HALL
Hat: JOHN CAVANAGH
Collar: WENTWORTH
Shirt: BERNARD WEATHERILL
Gloves: FOWNES
Helmets: HERBERT JOHNSON
Boots: HENRY MAXWELL

Right: Ann Bonfoey Taylor, 1967.

Mrs. Taylor remained in full riding habit, including false eyelashes throughout the afternoon as others slowly divested themselves of their boots and jackets.

"ACROSS THE PLAINS STRETCHES THE ORANGE COUNTY HUNT,"
WASHINGTON POST, NOVEMBER 5, 1967

The Taylors enjoyed participating in fox hunts and riding events in Virginia and England. Traditional sports of royalty, fox hunting and riding are steeped in a long history of established practice, which not only governs the rules of the sport but strictly regulates the proper attire. Ensembles such as this jacket and vest would have been worn during formal occasions. Taylor selected her riding clothes with the same discerning eye she brought to her collection of haute couture, choosing to work with only the best of the bespoke houses in London. These specialized tailors had the greatest understanding of the range of movement and durability riding attire required.

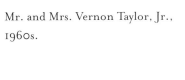

BERNARD WEATHERILL

(English)
Riding jacket, 1960s
Wool

Trousers: HARRY HALL
Shirt: BROOKS BROTHERS
Helmets: HERBERT JOHNSON
Boots: HENRY MAXWELL

Informal riding attire is usually made from neutral-colored cavalry twill, whipcord, tweed, or melton wool fabric. Pieces such as this jacket, commonly referred to as a hacking jacket or ratcatcher, would have been worn during casual riding sessions or early in the fox hunting season. Taylor rode extensively and had a number of outfits that were expertly cleaned and cared for by her and her staff. Dores, a house staff member for over thirty years, remembered, "We cleaned the boots every day after Mrs. Taylor was finished riding. She knew exactly how she wanted us to polish and store every item." Several closets in the Denver home were used to store different types of riding dress—one for Virginia fox hunting, another for English fox hunting, and yet another for everyday riding in Denver.

HERMÈS

(French)
Jacket, skirt, and sweater, late 1960s
Wool

Hat: JEAN-CHARLES BROSSEAU
Satchel: GUCCI
Boots: HENRY MAXWELL

It has been said of Hermès that it is perhaps the only establishment in the world in which one cannot buy a single article that is not in perfect taste.

"SPORT SUITS KEYED TO A FORMAL NOTE," NEW YORK TIMES, MAY 12, 1940

In the 1920s, building on its established reputation as a purveyor of luxury leather goods, Hermès introduced ready-to-wear clothes of superb quality for sports and travel. Portraying the lifestyle of the uppermost level of international society, advertisements promoted the elegant and comfortable clothes for hunting and golf, office and house, mountain and sea, travel and city.

Taylor's collection of sporting attire (seen on pages 54 through 59) includes a range of Hermès styles worn as complete ensembles and in combination with other custom-made pieces by luxury makers. She and Moose participated in shooting expeditions in England, Ireland, and Scotland with their circle of friends. Taylor shot with a 20-gauge side by side and also owned a matching pair of Purdey guns, and Moose fondly recalled, "She was a good shot!"

Custom-made cape and skirt, 1960s
Wool with fox pelt appliqué

Hat: HERBERT JOHNSON
Scarf: CARLO RAIMONDI
Sweater: N. PEAL
Boots: RENE MANCINI

HERMÈS

(French)
Cape and trousers, 1960s
Leather with cashmere lining and metal fixtures

Hat: TIROL
Sweater: DONNA KENDALL
Boots: HENRY MAXWELL

SCHNEIDERS

(Austrian)
Jacket, 1960s
Wool and cashmere

Skirt: HERMÈS "Boutique Sport"
Hat: DOLOMITONHUT
Scarf: HERMÈS
Sweater: S. FISHER
Bag: GUCCI
Boots: RENE MANCINI

HERMÈS

(French)
Jacket, belt, and trousers, 1960s
Wool

Hat: TISCHLER HUT
Sweater: HALSTON
Boots: HENRY MAXWELL

HERMÈS

(French)
Cape and trousers, 1960s
Wool with metallic closures

Sweater: W. BILL
Boots: HENRY MAXWELL

Ann Bonfoey Taylor and gamekeeper
hunting on her Denver estate, 1967.

HERMÈS

(French)
Sweater, 1960s
Wool

Skirt: HUBER SPORTMODEN
Hat: GELOT
Scarf: CHARVET
Blouse: DONNA KENDALL
Satchel: GIVENCHY
Boots: HENRY MAXWELL

BROOKS-VAN HORN

(American)

French hussar military costume, 1960s

Wool with gold metallic braid

BROOKS-VAN HORN

(American)

French military costume, 1960s

Wool, cotton, metal fixtures, and leather

BRETT

(American)

French military costume, 1960s

Wool

Military hats, crossbelts and pouches:

Various American and European styles, 19th–20th century

Taylor had a great interest in military uniforms and incorporated them into both her ski attire and the decor of her Denver and Vail homes. Maintaining a feminine silhouette with form-fitting jackets cinched at the waist, snug pants, and high boots, she often had her uniforms custom made or adapted so that they fit to her liking and were more practical to wear. Taylor was of Huguenot heritage, and her fascination with military grew out of her deep love of Europe and the United Kingdom, particularly the traditions of English royalty. Vail, which was modeled on a European-style village, was the perfect setting for her sensibilities. In this photograph, Taylor wears one of her military costumes in the hallway of her Vail home.

MABEL FURS

(American)
Coats, 1960s–1980s
Mongolian sheep
Lent by Ashley Taylor and Sheika Gramshammer

Left to right:
Boots: TECNICA
Glasses: CARRERA
Hat: MR. JOHN
Boots: JANPE
Glasses: HUNTING WORLD
Belt and pouch: HERMÈS

These striking coats, made from Mongolian sheep pelts, were custom designed for Taylor by Mabel Furs in Denver. Not only did they suit her bold style on the ski slopes, they were practical due to their light weight and exceptional warmth. While Taylor's well-known reputation for being a discerning woman of style was inspiring to many, it was intimidating to some. Sheika Gramshammer described the memorable experience of meeting Taylor for the first time: "I never had another woman check me out the way she did and although nervous inside, I just walked up to her and twirled around and asked her, 'Do you like what you see?'" Taken by her boldness, Taylor replied, "Yes!" and the two became fast friends. "Ann always used to call me 'my yellow bird.'" As a remembrance, Taylor gave this yellow coat to Gramshammer.

Ann Bonfoey Taylor, Vail, Colorado, 1967.

MARIANO FORTUNY

(Italian, born Spain, 1871-1949)

When asked what was his favorite dress his wife wore, Vernon Taylor, Jr., firmly replied, "Fortuny. The skirts were billowy and had a lot of pleats on them. And they were very, very becoming to her." This "Delphos" gown, based on Greek statuary, is Mariano Fortuny's best-known design, which he created in 1909 and produced in variation throughout his career, along with velvet jackets and gowns stenciled with medieval and Eastern motifs. At the time of its making, this dress was considered radically simplistic. Created solely from two long, rectangular pieces of masterfully hand-pleated delicate silk drawn in at the neckline, it has an incredibly fluid nature that completely depends on the wearer's body to give it shape and size. Taylor's youthful, athletic frame found a perfectly modern expression in the gown when she wore it mid-century. The romance of the classical references, the highly artistic design, and the painstaking craftsmanship contributed to her appreciation Fortuny's work.

Jacket and "Delphos" gown, 1920s–1930s. Jacket: silk and cotton velvet stenciled with metallic pigment; gown: silk.

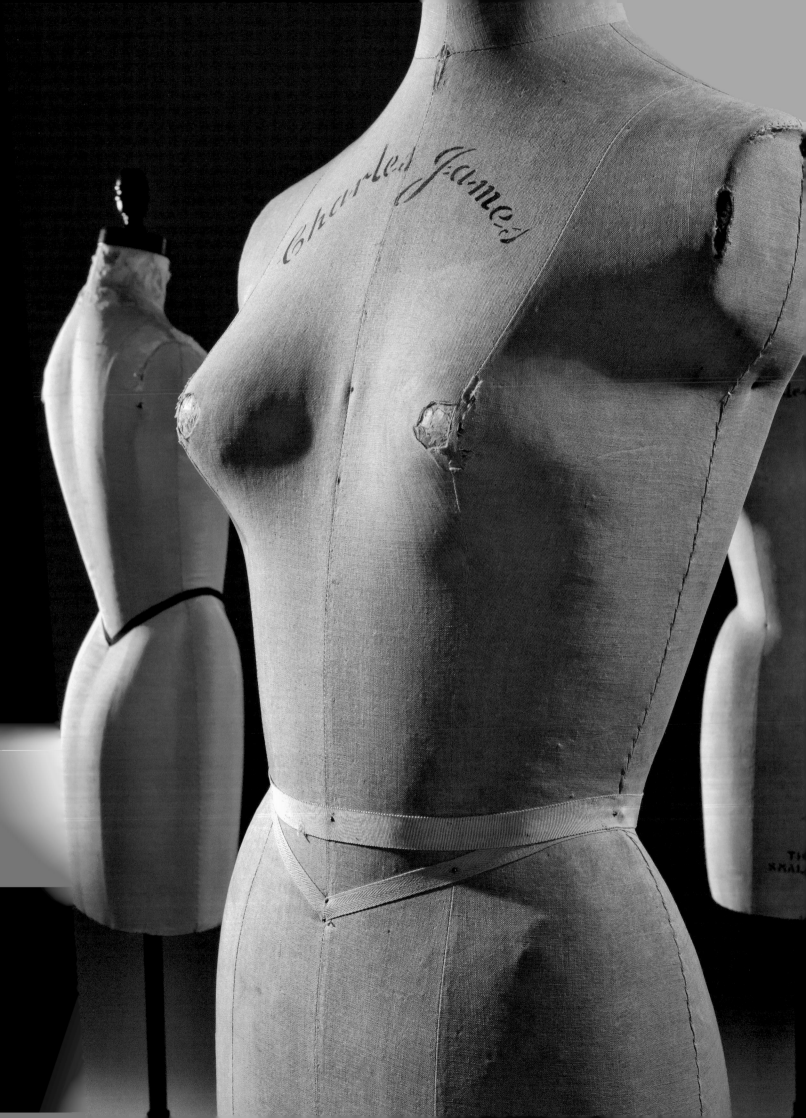

CHARLES JAMES

(American, born England, 1906-1978)

If I were known for only two things, it would be the celebrated displacement of the dart and the
wall of air between the body and the fabric.

CHARLES JAMES, SOHO WEEKLY NEWS, SEPTEMBER 28, 1978

Taylor had a number of coats, suits, and gowns custom made by Charles James from 1949 through 1953. Notoriously fickle and sometimes ill-tempered, James only made clothes for women he liked and who possessed a presence and figure he appreciated. Taylor's slim body, athletic grace, and keen understanding of design fit his ideal. Working with James established Taylor as one of the best dressed and most distinguished tastemakers of the era.

Taylor's wardrobe reveals that she was self-assured, even in her earliest couture choices. She selected some of James's most austere, sculptural works, predominated by the color gray, including a number of understated day clothes. These extraordinary examples of James's daywear are very rare and certainly a highlight of the collection.

James created custom-designed dress forms based on his concept of the ideal contemporary shape. A dipped waistline and flat derrière emphasize a long curving line at the back, and, at the front, a high, small bustline, pulled back shoulders, and forward-thrusting hips create an erect posture. The clothes in this section were all photographed on original Charles James forms with the exception of the "La Sirène" gowns, which depend on the legs of the mannequin for their shape. The dating and captions were produced with the advice and consultation of Homer Layne, a trusted assistant to Charles James for eight years.

Original Charles James dress forms. Metal and silk; metal and cotton. Collection of Phoenix Art Museum and Collection of Stephens College, Columbia, Missouri.

Vogue, August 15, 1954.

CHARLES JAMES

Coat and belt, 1954
Wool with wool jersey lining

CHARLES JAMES

"Chesterfield" coat, 1952
Wool with silk lining

A coat cut somewhat along the line of a gentleman's coat circa 1810. It cleaves to the body as though the marvelous cashmere were molten, a torrent of cloth gripped at the small of the back with a shaped belt. The set of the collar, the armholes is an aesthetic delight.

HARPER'S BAZAAR, JULY 1951

Although he was most celebrated for his magnificent ball gowns, James also created dramatic and exceptionally tailored daywear and coats. The silhouette of these two coats lends the fashionable appearance of a backward swaying upper torso with hips thrust forward. In addition to studying the human form, James researched the cut and fit of historical garments to arrive at his originally shaped clothing. The "Chesterfield" coat was inspired by a popular men's overcoat. The shaped side front edge creates the illusion of a smaller waist, as does the curve of the belt at center back. Long darts in the front and James's specialized Z-cut side back seams shape the fabric to the upper body with the smoothest and cleanest line possible. The hips are exaggerated by heavy interlinings and diagonal pockets. In the checked coat, the integration of a hood is very unique. It is possible this feature was made at Taylor's request based on her affinity for wearing them while skiing. The hood is lined in wool jersey, a fabric Taylor often used to make head wraps to wear under hats.

CHARLES JAMES

"Cossack" coat, 1951

Artillery twill wool

ANTONIO LOPEZ

Illustration, early 1970s

India ink on paper

Artillery twill, a substantial cloth that takes shape. Mr. James uses it to shape the Louis Philippe sleeve (hitherto he has done this sleeve only in satin or taffeta) of a short-jacket suit.

HARPER'S BAZAAR, JULY 1951

This coat is an outstanding example of James's pure sculptural forms. Its extreme simplicity—even the buttons are hidden—reveals the integrity of its geometric seams. James based this trademark arc-sleeved coat on a Civil War uniform in his personal collection. He adapted the uniform's curved, two-piece sleeve with grand gesture and the aid of an architect's compass. The highly unconventional placement of spiral metal boning on the inside of the armscye holds the seam arc straight out to the side. Gussets incorporated into the under sleeves provide a range of movement with the high close armhole and allow the waist to become tightly fitted. The hips are exaggerated by heavily padded horsehair interlinings and low set-in pockets with flaps.

Illustrator Antonio Lopez collaborated with James in the late 1960s and early 1970s to document the masterworks of the designer's career. After the drawings were displayed in an exhibition at the Everson Museum of Art in Syracuse, New York, in 1975, James gifted them to several institutions, including Phoenix Art Museum. This particular illustration depicts a variation of the "Cossack" coat with a visible button at the waist.

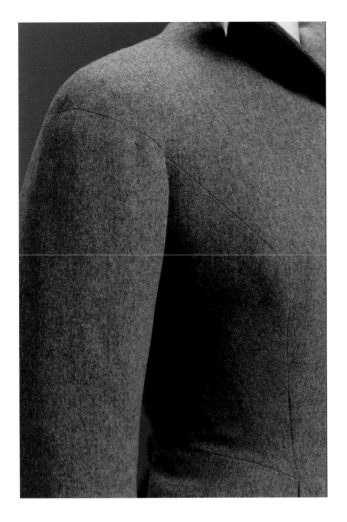
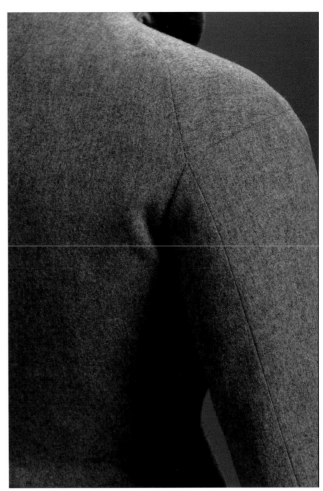

CHARLES JAMES

"Dressmaker" suit (jacket and "Dorothy" skirt), 1951
Wool flannel

You wouldn't think anybody could spend $20,000 on a sleeve—you know, a sleeve, the thing you put your arm into.
But Charlie James did it. . . . It is, he says, a revolutionary sleeve. It has one inch more than the usual amount of
material in it. A woman can move her arm in this sleeve, he says. Or shrug her shoulders, he says. Or pitch a baseball.
All without dislocating her waistline, bunching at the collar, or splitting a gusset.

"YOUNG MAN OF FASHION," COLLIER'S, SEPTEMBER 29, 1947

In the 1947 fashion collections, the heavy shoulder padding of women's war-era suits was removed in favor of
a softer, more feminine look. James made and tested hundreds of sleeves in his effort to achieve such structural
change, and this suit is the result of his painstaking pursuit to create an original proportion for the postwar
silhouette. Like the "Cossack" coat on page 70, it represents Taylor's preference for the designer's sleekest form
in a substantial fabric.

A bone runs along the center front of the jacket above the hidden button closure, keeping the line perfectly
smooth. Additionally, the shaped center front line is neat and straight when fastened. The jacket is paired with
the "Dorothy" skirt, which features oblique tucks in the front and a deep overlap in back for ease of movement.
Narrow but not straight, the skirt has shaped side seams that impart a slight roundness to the hips.

CHARLES JAMES

Dress, 1953
Wool jersey

This dress incorporates several design elements that Taylor favored in other garments by James she had previously ordered. It features a softer variation of the signature arcing sleeve on the "Cossack" coat (see page 70). The skirt displays the style of center front pleating seen on the "Dorothy" skirt (see page 73), and the angled welt pockets are similar to those on the "Chesterfield" coat (see page 69).

James used varying techniques to maintain the overall sleekness of this garment despite the substantial weight of the wool jersey fabric. The gusset is incorporated into the under sleeve, reducing the bulk a traditional triangular would have made. Center front and back seams eliminate side seams and keep the skirt smooth over the hipline.

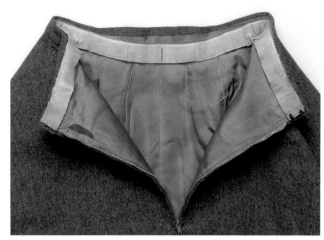

CHARLES JAMES

Bolero jacket and skirt, 1951
Wool with silk lining
Wool flannel

The inside of this bolero jacket features a fabric-covered elastic band that allows the back to swing away from the body. James executed an arcing line not only in the sleeves but all along the jacket front and stand-out collar. Sleek, angled princess seams create a second arc that stretches from the jacket front to the armscye. James often lined jackets in vibrant silk taffeta (in this case, deep rose) to add an element of surprise.

James used just two pieces of fabric to create the extraordinary shape of this full skirt, adding layers of interfacing to build up its structural form. Interfacing not only gives emphasis to the hip but enhances the three-dimensionality of the unpressed pleats. A precisely sewn double welt pocket hidden in the side pleat provides entry into an oversize pocket underneath. The shaped waistband is paired with a grosgrain waist stay stabilizer, which provided support and helped keep the garment in place. Together, the two pieces create the illusion of a small, tight waistline.

CHARLES JAMES

Theatre coat, c. 1950
Silk matelasse

CHARLES JAMES

"Infanta" late-day dress, c. 1950
Silk and cotton velvet with silk organza
underlining

For November premieres, when the theatre is at its brightest and best short but grand outfits—planned for public appearances. The theatre coat in heavy black Catoir satin, street length with a sharp in and out shape . . . by Charles James, made to order.

HARPER'S BAZAAR, NOVEMBER 1949

Both glamorous and useful for varied occasions, this black velveteen dress and the black silk coat dress on the previous two pages served as wardrobe staples for Taylor's cosmopolitan evenings out in New York or abroad.

Waist stays inside the coat support the weight of the skirt, keeping the bodice in place. The dress has spiral boning over the bustline and in the bodice to keep the broad sweetheart neckline smooth. The voluminous eight-gore skirt has an organza underlining to give it movement and a touch of buoyancy.

CHARLES JAMES

"La Sirène" evening dresses, 1952
Silk crepe

CECIL BEATON

A Sunday-morning View of the Dressmaking
Workroom at Elizabeth Arden's.
Vogue, December 15, 1944

Poise, posture, and correct proportions are necessary for any modern fashion. And these are assets which seldom come delivered in a neat little package . . . you have to earn them the hard way.

"CUSTOM-MADE FIGURES FOR CUSTOM-MADE CLOTHES," VOGUE, DECEMBER 15, 1944

Already the head of an incredibly successful cosmetics company, Elizabeth Arden opened a fashion business within her beauty salon in 1943 and hired Charles James as one of her designers. This Cecil Beaton sketch of Arden's workroom shows a variation of one of James's best-known designs, "La Sirène," in the process of being draped. The dress was originally designed for Mrs. Oliver Burr Jennings in 1938, and Taylor was one of at least seven additional women, including Gypsy Rose Lee, Doris Duke, and Elizabeth Arden, who had this design made for her with various neckline and sleeve treatments between 1938 and 1957.

Cut on the cross grain, the skirt is horizontally tucked in gradation from top to bottom with double tucks for volume over the hips. The gathering captures the fullness along the center back seam and forms an alluring fishtail back. Ever discerning and apt to make alterations, Taylor had the long sleeves on the black dress added in later years.

CHARLES JAMES

Ball gown, bodice, and evening coat, 1949
Gown and bodice: silk taffeta and duchess
satin; coat: silk taffeta

With his genius for creating new forms in fabric, Charles James . . . fashions an evening gown—a brilliant
abstraction of the rose that in every artful inch contributes a dynamic grace to the female figure. The rib-tight
bodice . . . unfurls about the shoulders in an effect of rose petals.

FLAIR, MAY 1950

One of only a few known matching sets, this ball gown, bodice, and evening coat epitomize the grand
eveningwear James is best known for. Their timeless beauty lies in the precision of their construction, sculptural
shape, and beautiful coloring, all of which combine to give these pieces classical stature.

    Although it appears deceptively simple in design, the gown is created from layers of nylon under-linings,
pads, and ruffles, which James used to build up its structural form. The gown and bodice are also a study in
James's expert use of draping and juxtaposition of different grain lines to achieve various effects. In the over
bodice, one continuous piece of fabric creates the arc across the décolletage, the sleeve, and the upper bodice
back. In the dress, bows neaten the transition point of the shoulder strap and bodice, and, when the over bodice
is worn, they intersect perfectly to become part of its harmonious sculptural flow. In the coat, oblique double box
pleats on the sleeves fall open to create grand volume and a graceful teardrop shape.

JAMES GALANOS

(American, born 1925)

One of the great American designers, James Galanos was held in the highest regard for the contemporary feel and supreme workmanship of his clothes. This dress is designed to be both comfortable and stylish. Its closely fitted bodice is complemented by the buoyant fullness of the skirt, which Galanos achieved through deep pleats at center front and back, double box pleats on each side, and four-quarter circle gores at side fronts and backs. The combination of pleats and gores gives the skirt a pleasing undulation.

Taylor's good friend Harriett Kelly remembered a spontaneous visit they once made to Galanos's Los Angeles studio: "In the late 1950s and into the 1960s, my husband was an executive at Continental Airlines and Bob Six was the CEO. We had all been at a party and Ann mentioned wanting to see James Galanos. Bob said, 'Why don't you girls go out there?' So the next morning we took a plane to Los Angeles. Galanos and his crew provided us with a lovely lunch and fashion show. Ann tried on everything and she looked fabulous in everything. She really looked at clothes like a collector looks at paintings. She had fashion on her mind no matter what she was doing. Every time I saw her she looked absolutely fabulous."

Dress, early 1960s. Wool knit.

CRISTÓBAL BALENCIAGA

(Spanish, 1895–1972)

It has been said of Cristóbal Balenciaga that he is "the da Vinci" of the couture, "the Molière of dressmakers." American designers have said that viewing his collections is like "attending the Sorbonne," and his fellow couturiers refer to him as "the master." All of these expressions are just other ways of describing M. Balenciaga. He is the greatest dress designer in the world today.

NEW YORK TIMES, SEPTEMBER 1, 1958

Cristóbal Balenciaga was indisputably considered the master designer of his era—a designer's designer. Coco Chanel once said that he was one of the only couturiers left in Paris who could make a garment from start to finish completely by himself. While Chanel suits were the prevailing attire among the luncheon set during the 1960s, women of utmost distinction arrived in Balenciaga. Understated and discreet, his clothes are superb examples of perfect cut and proportion.

Taylor chose Balenciaga because he was the best and she appreciated the clothes down to the essence of their details. Her selections show a steady commitment to Balenciaga's classic designs from the late 1950s through the close of his house in 1968. She shied away from the designer's more outrageous or conservative works in favor of pieces that epitomize her consistent meter of style—timeless and sophisticated but with great flair. The detail of this coat highlights Balenciaga's signature darted semi-fitted front and perfectly proportioned all-in-one sleeve. These touches add a distinctly feminine look to the silhouette, which is inspired by a classic men's overcoat.

The clothes in this section are organized chronologically by the year they were made. These groupings do not document everything Taylor purchased during each particular year; rather, they demonstrate selections of what has survived and come to the Museum. The exact dating and fabric descriptions were made possible by the gracious assistance of Marie-Andrée Jouve, archivist at Balenciaga for over thirty years, who also contributed valuable information on Taylor's personal *vendeuse*.

Detail of coat (see page 98).

Ann Bonfoey Taylor was an extraordinary woman who, although athletic, had extreme elegance. She dressed herself simply in distinguished, neutral tones, with lots of gray for every day. Her charming personality and presence were so grand that she could select restrained colors and still look elegant because she wore the clothes so well. Her preference for designs with spare, clean lines was very sage and reasonable because of their versatility and timelessness. Although other women ordered more clothes, Mrs. Taylor's choices were of the most thoughtful nature.

—JEANINE, TAYLOR'S PERSONAL BALENCIAGA VENDEUSE

Wearing a little gray Balenciaga suit and quite marvelous eyelashes she is eating a quick breakfast in her suite at the Carlyle. Since she is lighting there only temporarily—she just flew in from Paris the night before—there are eleven pieces of elegant, Vuitton luggage in the background, Vuitton is so sturdy and it was wonderful in Uganda last summer, she says.

"INSIDE FASHION: NEVER A RED SKI PARKA," NEW YORK HERALD TRIBUNE, OCTOBER 4, 1965

CRISTÓBAL BALENCIAGA

Dress, c. 1959   Suit (jacket and skirt), 1959
Gerondeau wool crepe   Lahondes wool

The curved kimono sleeve, the master's brilliant innovation in a bias-cut construction producing a deep
shadow fold, and revealing the body as it moves within . . . . destined for many encores.

"BALENCIAGA'S PROPHECY," HARPER'S BAZAAR, MAY 1959

Balenciaga was at the peak of his trendsetting influence during the 1959 season, when Taylor added
these two gray day ensembles and matching coat and dress to her wardrobe. Sleeves were of paramount
importance to Balenciaga, and he devoted a great deal of time and effort to their perfection. Both of the
day ensembles demonstrate the curved kimono sleeve Balenciaga introduced in his collections that year.
The sleeves of the dress are cut in one piece with the body so that the grain of the fabric is on bias, which
allowed for comfortable ease of movement.

CRISTÓBAL BALENCIAGA

Coat and dress, 1959
Silk faille

CRISTÓBAL BALENCIAGA

Evening dress and coat, 1962–63
Abraham silk

From the illusive Mr. Balenciaga himself come no predictions. Our own feelings are distilled from twenty-five years of close and admiring attention to this unusual fashion personality, sometimes called the "the couturier's couturier," who designs two years ahead of everyone else. Expected: insight always sways, sometimes turns the tide of fashion; elegance no matter what the silhouette; distinction, no matter what direction it may take.

"FOR 25 YEARS FASHION'S MOST PERVADING INFLUENCE BALENCIAGA," HARPER'S BAZAAR, JULY 1962

The July 1962 issue of *Harper's Bazaar* featured a cover story and twelve-page editorial saluting the twenty-five year anniversary of Balenciaga's couture house. Editor-in-chief Carmel Snow had long been an eloquent and constant champion of the designer, foreseeing the impact his work would have on the rest of fashion.

This dress and coat are a culmination of Balenciaga's classic elements: sleeves cut from one piece with the body, utilizing bias for ease and comfort; a bias-cut bodice that emphasizes the curves of the body; a high waistline with plenty of gathers to create a flattering roundness. The photograph by Toni Frissell, taken at a personal photo shoot in 1971, depicts Taylor in the coat nearly ten years after she purchased it.

CRISTÓBAL BALENCIAGA

Coat, mid-1960s

Wool

. . . cut with the effortless certainty true simplicity exacts. . .

HARPER'S BAZAAR, OCTOBER 1963

Although this long, narrow, double-breasted coat was inspired by a classic men's overcoat, the semi-fitted front and curved shoulder line give it a distinctly feminine look. The exquisite geometrical construction consists of distinctly divided, perfectly proportioned planes that combine to create sleek volume, reminiscent of the clean lines prevalent in mid-century modern architecture.

CRISTÓBAL BALENCIAGA

Suit (jacket and skirt), 1964–65
Wool

Suit (jacket and dress), 1964
Wool

Suit (jacket and skirt), 1963
Garigue wool

The suits of Balenciaga are the definitive suits of this time, their silhouette now reflected across Paris. This year . . .
the suit is in closer collaboration with the woman's body, the jacket near in front, within an ace of being fitted
in the back.

"CARMEL SNOW'S REPORT," HARPER'S BAZAAR, SEPTEMBER 1952

Balenciaga set the look of the most popular suit silhouette from the mid-1950s to the mid-1960s. Widely copied by other designers and mass manufacturers, the semi-fitted front and loose back design he originated in the early 1950s broke from the stronghold of Christian Dior's pinched waist New Look silhouette of 1947. Balenciaga's unconfined shape complimented a wider range of figures and better served the more active, modern lifestyle of women during the 1960s.

In these four suits he designed for Taylor, Balenciaga utilized subtle yet complementary variations—such as differing darts and seaming on the sleeves—to enhance the quality of the fabrics and add uniqueness to individual pieces while retaining the basic suit silhouette. Gathers below the waistbands of the skirts add a desirable amount of ease and roundness to the hipline. While Balenciaga's suits are always decidedly feminine, they often include pockets, belts, and other tailoring details borrowed from menswear.

CRISTÓBAL BALENCIAGA
Suit (jacket and skirt), 1963
Gerondeau wool

CRISTÓBAL BALENCIAGA

Evening dress, 1964
Lamarre silk duchess satin

Watching a Balenciaga fitting was like watching a miracle: when you saw his dresses, they didn't seem to have been touched. They floated, they moved, they created mystery.

HUBERT DE GIVENCHY

This princess-line dress was one of the most elegant, timeless garments a woman could own, and its ability to be worn with many different types of jewelry or accessories also made it incredibly versatile. Like a well-designed automobile, chair, or any other work of sculptural design, this dress derives it beauty from the perfection of its lines and proportion. Minimalism requires the maximum skill and quality materials—the true essence of couture, something at which Balenciaga was a master.

CRISTÓBAL BALENCIAGA

Suit (jacket and skirt), winter 1967
Nattier wool

Coat, 1967
Nattier wool and wool with silk
velvet collar

Opposite:
Dress, 1967
Lajoinie silk

These garments are some of Balenciaga's final designs before he closed his couture house in 1968. By the late 1960s, the world and fashion along with it had changed tremendously, and the emerging youth-oriented culture favored the less expensive and trend-driven styles of ready-to-wear collections. In his last several seasons, Balenciaga tried to include youthful elements—such as the pink color of this coat—in his clothes. Ultimately, however, he could not bear to give up his high standards of precise workmanship and refused to introduce a commercial line, choosing to close rather than compromise. An adaptation of a Balenciaga classic first introduced in 1957, this baby doll dress features a fully boned inner corset to keep the garment correctly positioned on the body.

HUBERT DE GIVENCHY

(French, born 1927)

True couture is not a matter of taking a bit of chiffon and sewing a flower on it; rather, it is knowing how to construct a lining on the bias.

HUBERT DE GIVENCHY

In 1952, at age twenty-four, Hubert de Givenchy opened his fashion house in Paris. After Cristóbal Balenciaga, he was considered the most important couturier of the late 1950s and 1960s. Balenciaga was also Givenchy's closest friend and mentor, and the two designers stood stoically outside the mainstream fashion system at its pinnacle. Unlike other houses, who showed their designs to the press simultaneously over the span of a week, Balenciaga and Givenchy held their shows nearly a month later to prevent copyists from manufacturing and selling knock-offs before their clients had a chance to order and receive originals. This required the fashion editors to make two trips to Paris to cover their shows, which speaks to the influence these two great designers had.

Like Balenciaga, Givenchy's designs epitomize elegant understatement, superb workmanship, and excellence of cut and proportion. Organized, disciplined, and supremely attune to the details of clothing, Taylor shared many of Givenchy's points of view and interests, including his love of nature and especially flowers. Several of Taylor's Givenchy garments feature floral brocades and embroideries, always set on a solid foundation of cut and shape. The detail of the cocktail jacket at left shows a rolled collar—a Givenchy signature.

Detail of jacket (see page III).

HUBERT DE GIVENCHY

Suit (jacket and skirt), 1960s
Wool

Suit (jacket, dress, and belt), 1960s
Wool

*Discreet, well-defined, articulate—the commanding simplicity of Givenchy's perfect cut. Superb black dress . . .
arrow-narrow, its waistline a lowered arc in back.*

"GIVENCHY: BRILLIANT, TAUT TAILORING," VOGUE, NOVEMBER 1963

Givenchy used concave front darts and straight back seams to create the signature semi-fitted front and loose
back shape of these ensembles. He achieved additional ease in the bodice of the dress by hanging the skirt on
an inner silk bodice, leaving the over panel to fall gently from the shoulders. Gathering softens the skirt line
emphasizing a feminine roundness in the silhouette. This look became part of an international vocabulary
of grace and allure in the early 1960s that was widely popularized by Givenchy's clients such as First Lady
Jacqueline Kennedy and by Audrey Hepburn in many movies, most prominently *Breakfast at Tiffany's* (1961).

HUBERT DE GIVENCHY

Dress, early 1960s
Silk

HUBERT DE GIVENCHY

Coat, 1960s
Embroidered wool

HUBERT DE GIVENCHY

Cocktail suit (jacket, dress, and belt), 1960s
Silk brocade

HUBERT DE GIVENCHY
Cocktail coat and dress, 1960s
Silk

HUBERT DE GIVENCHY

Cocktail coat
Silk satin, 1960s

From Balenciaga and Givenchy, this season's triumphant view of an unfailing dedication to line, to taste, to simplicity, to elegance. These are clothes to be worn with the courage of fashion conviction, their most arresting attribute, a complete lack of adornment.

HARPER'S BAZAAR, NOVEMBER 1963

The expressive power of this long coat demonstrates Givenchy's extraordinary understanding of fabric and the shaping that can be achieved by cutting it on different angles of the grain. The diagonal seam running from the center front bustline to the lower third at center back serves as the dividing line for Givenchy's alternating use of straight and bias grain pieces. At front, bias cut aids in molding the fabric over the bust, and straight grain creates the defined volume below. At back, straight grain above the seam allows the back to fall loosely from the shoulders and meet bias grain below the seam for a soft flourish in the volume of the back.

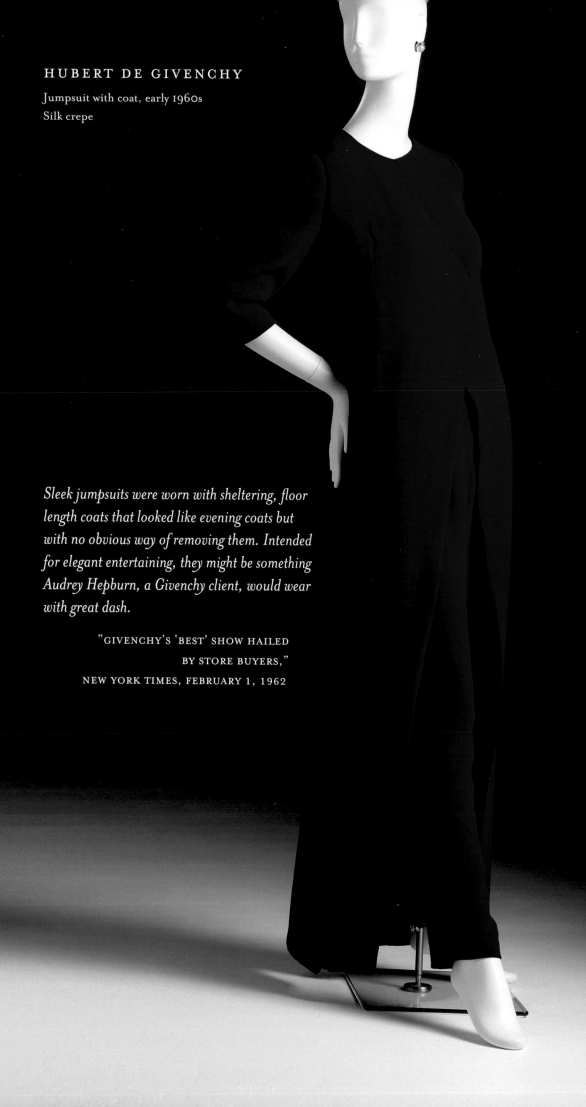

HUBERT DE GIVENCHY

Jumpsuit with coat, early 1960s
Silk crepe

*Sleek jumpsuits were worn with sheltering, floor
length coats that looked like evening coats but
with no obvious way of removing them. Intended
for elegant entertaining, they might be something
Audrey Hepburn, a Givenchy client, would wear
with great dash.*

"GIVENCHY'S 'BEST' SHOW HAILED
BY STORE BUYERS,"
NEW YORK TIMES, FEBRUARY 1, 1962

HUBERT DE GIVENCHY
Evening coat and dress with purse, 1960s
Silk cloqué

HUBERT DE GIVENCHY

Evening coat, 1960s
Silk satin shantung with silk organza
floral embroidery

Givenchy's collection is a Midsummer-Night's Dream: poetic, brimming with youth, full of ideas. There are beautiful prints like flowers seen under water. . . . More flowers alight on a lock of hair, the shoulders, the bosom, on ribbons, organdie fichues . . .

HARPER'S BAZAAR, MARCH 1954

A nature lover—especially of flowers—Givenchy found inspiration in its colors and motifs throughout his career. In the fabric of this coat, carnations are exquisitely sculpted from organza in great relief. Givenchy utilized embroidery as an enhancement of, never a substitute for, perfect proportion and line in a design. The designer believed "the more elaborate the fabric, the simpler the shape." A voluminous smock, this coat has a full cut back that swings from a yoke, showing off the field of flowers to full advantage.

HUBERT DE GIVENCHY

Evening coat and dress, early 1960s
Gazar and ostrich feathers with silk organza lining

The austere shape of this coat and dress is enlivened by the skirt's fluttering border of stripped and dyed ostrich feathers. Individually applied at alternating angles to give undulation and bounce, the feathers continue on the inside hemline to complete the effect when the wearer is seated. Although majestic in appearance, this ensemble is exceptionally lightweight. A silk organza lining finishes off the inside of the coat in the lightest possible manner without weighing down the buoyant hand of the gazar.

MADAME GRÈS (ALIX BARTON)

(French, 1903–1993)

Madame Grès approached her designs with the passion of a true artist. In the mid-1960s, when ready-to-wear collections were rapidly gaining popularity, Grès remained devoted to haute couture and continued to personally drape every style on a mannequin until the end of her career. "Grès had a way of draping and handling soft fabrics. She drew something out of it that others couldn't, and Ann had an appreciation and an understanding of that," remembers Taylor's friend, Robin Chandler Duke.

From 1965 through the 1970s, Grès developed an American clientele by showing her collections annually at the Musicians Emergency Fund charity luncheon in New York. Taylor was among those who attended and ordered designs, which were made in Paris and shipped back to New York. In 1979 the *New York Times* reported,

"A Grès design is not an ephemeral fancy but a long-term investment. Some 30 American clients have long held this view, some coming from as far as Chicago, Denver and Los Angeles to place their orders with the Grès entourage during their four-day New York visit." Additionally, Taylor visited Grès's couture house on her regular trips to Paris.

Taylor's distinctive selection of Grès daywear and evening gowns demonstrates her adventuresome, original taste. Drawn to more than just the designer's signature Grecian inspired gowns, Taylor explored a refined and discreet range of Grès's work in the 1960s and early 1970s.

Detail of jacket (see page 124).

MADAME GRÈS (ALIX BARTON)

Coat, 1960s
Double-faced wool

Coat and dress with belt, mid-1960s
Double-faced wool and wool jersey

Double-faced wool, below—one of a rave of excellent little reversible coats at Grès. Half downy white fleece . . . ,
half crisp grey twill. With a smooth flat back, welt seams. Sleeves all-of-a-piece with a square back yoke.

VOGUE, MARCH 15, 1963

In these seemingly simple, elegant day coats, Grès demonstrated the flexibility and breadth of her talent. While many clients chose to purchase the designer's signature draped and pleated evening gowns, Taylor's selection of these refined, discreet day ensembles shows her sophisticated taste.

Both coats are made of double-faced wool, which requires advanced technical skill to maintain a clean, perfect finish. Because all edges and seams may be finished off neatly, the coats do not require linings and therefore remain light and supple. The detail on page 122 of the green coat's bound buttonhole shows the conviction of Grès's standards of perfection in the use of this extraordinary fabric.

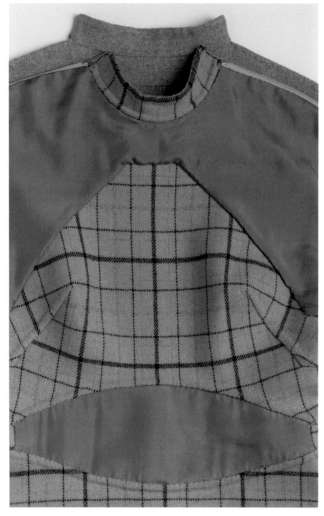

MADAME GRÈS (ALIX BARTON)

Dress, 1960s
Wool jersey

Dress, 1960s
Double-faced wool and leather with silk partial lining

These deceptively simple day dresses not only have an exclusive elegance, they are designed to be comfortable to wear and to feel good against the body. Although her work is marked by continuity, Grès felt it was important that fashion follow the changing times. From the mid-1960s and especially in the 1970s, her garments began to reflect the evolution toward more casual clothes. Taylor's strong preference for discreet and refined luxury finds its ultimate expression in these dresses, which she appreciated for their comfortable elegance and their ability to move in pace with her active lifestyle.

MADAME GRÈS (ALIX BARTON)

Dress, 1960s
Silk crepe

Dress, 1960s
Silk crepe

Grès designs seem sensual. Her femininity is always asserted in dresses—jersey or bias-cut crepe—that curve over the body and beautify it.

NEW YORK TIMES, FEBRUARY 2, 1965

These feminine dresses find form in the superior cut and drape of the fabric on the body. The fluid pleating in the skirt of the blue dress adds three-dimensionality, which is balanced by the clean lines of the bodice. The black dress relies on bias cut to gracefully flute the fabric around the body. Understated and refined, these dresses undoubtedly accentuated Taylor's graceful elegance and poise.

MADAME GRÈS (ALIX BARTON)

Dress and hooded coat, late 1960s
Angora jersey

With great dexterity, Grès managed to adapt to the pulse of changing times while maintaining her own identifiable style. During the late 1960s through the 1970s, she created couture-level sportswear that was in step with the era's more casual lifestyle. Using bold geometric shapes, Grès draped ensembles and long gowns from soft angora jersey in silhouettes with great volume. Simple in form but made of exquisite fabric, this hooded coat and dress have an elegant but relaxed timelessness that made them incredibly versatile to wear, as demonstrated by the photograph of Taylor on the beach, which was taken during a personal photo shoot with Toni Frissell in 1971.

MADAME GRÈS
(ALIX BARTON)

Evening gown, late 1960s–early 1970s
Silk taffeta

MADAME GRÈS
(ALIX BARTON)

Evening gown,
mid-1960s–early 1970s
Silk velvet and silk jersey

To maintain the perfection
of this columnar couture
dress, its closure has been
carved along the shoulder,
neckline, and side bodice,
fastened by a long line of
alternating hooks and eyes
and snaps.

MADAME GRÈS (ALIX BARTON)

Evening gown and wrap, 1960s
Matte silk jersey

Madame Grès' name is almost synonymous with jersey. There is no other designer in the world who can take this fabric and shape it, tuck it and drape it as she can. Everyone always waits impatiently to see her Helen of Troy evening gowns.

"FASHION TRENDS ABROAD," NEW YORK TIMES, JANUARY 31, 1959

From her start in 1938 to her retirement fifty years later, Grès evolved her signature classically inspired gowns to reflect the lifestyle changes of each decade. The initial gowns are fluid, unstructured designs that entail many yards of fabric draped and pleated around the body. Her postwar versions are more structured, with precisely manipulated pleats individually sewn down onto organza foundations with boning and padding. The foundations allowed Grès to cut away sections of the dress and to condense the bodice to its sleekest form.

This variation of Grès's classic gown is made from rectangles of tissue-thin silk jersey. The dress is completely devoid of waist seams; each skirt panel runs straight up to the bodice and is condensed and manipulated across to the shoulder point. Grès used additional partial panels to fill out the remaining areas of the bodice.

MADAME GRÈS (ALIX BARTON)

Evening gown, late 1960s–early 1970s
Silk faille

Front entrance to the Taylors' Denver home, 1967.

Taylor favored Grès's evening gowns in various shades of green. Dresses like this one would not only compliment her coloring but were perfect backdrops for her emerald jewelry. Her eldest son, Vernon III, remembers coming home from school with a friend one afternoon to find his mother wearing this gown and her jewels. No special occasion was planned; Taylor had dressed up simply for the joy of it. While very romantic, this gown—with its dropped waist in perfect proportion to the length of the skirt—was also incredibly flattering to Taylor's figure.

MADAME GRÈS (ALIX BARTON)

Evening gown, mid-1960s
Silk satin with chinchilla cuffs

Madame Grès is one of those rare designers whose work transcends time, possibly because she is more interested in art than in trends. She creates forms and shapes and uses color with a painter's eye.

"MME. GRÈS: THE ART OF FASHION," NEW YORK TIMES, SEPTEMBER 19, 1980

Grès personally draped each of the styles in her collections, working directly with the fabric to refine her ideas. The elegance of this pure sculptural gown derives from the perfection of its silhouette, which Grès created by draping cut geometric pattern pieces on a mannequin. The deep folds of satin add to the garment's grand expression and reveal the designer's eye for chiaroscuro. In this photograph from a 1967 *Vogue* editorial shoot, Taylor wears the dress in the hallway of her Denver home.

Mr. and Mrs. Vernon Taylor, Jr., and sons, 1965.

We are pleased to have donated the masterfully
selected collection of haute couture and sporting
ensembles of our beloved wife and mother, who
was a uniquely stylish and elegantly athletic woman.

—VERNON TAYLOR, JR., AND FAMILY

Taylor family portrait. 1953
Douglas, Diane, Vernon Jr., Vernon III, Ann, Robert, and Jay.

CREDITS

Unless otherwise noted, all photographs of Ann Bonfoey Taylor's collection were taken by Ken Howie.

Frontispiece and pages 26, 32–33, 38, 42–45, 96, 131: Photos by Toni Frissell/Courtesy of the Taylor family.

Pages 8, 27–29, 46–47, 51, 58, 61, 63, 137–38, 140: Photos by Toni Frissell/Courtesy of Library of Congress, Prints and Photos Division, Toni Frissell Collection.

Page 10: Photo by Edward Steichen. *Vogue*, Aug. 1, 1933/Courtesy of Condé Nast Archive. Copyright © Condé Nast.

Pages 13, 22, 24, 39, 53, 55, 141: Courtesy of the Taylor family.

Page 14: Photo by Ralph Vincent/Courtesy of the Taylor family.

Page 15: *Harper's Bazaar*, Mar. 1, 1941/Courtesy of U.S. *Harper's Bazaar*.

Page 16: *Harper's Bazaar*, Feb. 1943/Courtesy of U.S. *Harper's Bazaar*.

Page 17: Photo by Ann Simpkins/Courtesy of the Taylor family.

Page 18: Left: *Harper's Bazaar*, Jan. 1946/Courtesy of U.S. *Harper's Bazaar*; right: original ski advertisement Courtesy of the Taylor family.

Page 19: Photos by B. Worsinger/Courtesy of the Taylor family.

Pages 20–21: Photos by Louise Dahl-Wolfe/Courtesy of the Taylor family.

Page 23: Left: Courtesy of the Taylor family; right: Photo by Hilton G. Hill/Courtesy of the Taylor family.

Page 25: Photo by Slim Aarons. *Holiday*, Mar. 1, 1964, Editorial #107581251 Mrs. Vernon Taylor by: Slim Aarons, Premium Archive.

Pages 30–31: Photos by Stan Rumbough.

Page 69: *Vogue*, Aug. 15, 1954/Courtesy of Condé Nast Archive. Copyright © Condé Nast.

Page 83: *Vogue*, Dec. 15, 1944/Courtesy of Condé Nast Archive. Copyright © Condé Nast.

Page 93: Photo by Morris Warman. *New York Herald Tribune*, Oct. 4, 1965/Courtesy of *New York Times*/Redux.

ACKNOWLEDGMENTS

Early in 2008, I received a telephone call from Vernon Taylor III, who modestly suggested that the Museum might be interested in some of his mother's wardrobe. Upon arriving at the Taylors' Denver home, I was led upstairs to an immense cedar walk-in closet. Opening the first drawer, I was astonished to find a significant and rare Charles James day coat, and I quickly knew I was in the presence of something extraordinary. First and foremost, I would like to thank Vernon "Moose" Taylor, Jr., for opening his home to accommodate the research and selection of the collection, and for his efforts to recount events that enliven our understanding of Taylor and her style. Vernon Taylor III also played an invaluable role, coordinating the donation and kindly providing endless counsel and insight. Special thanks also go to Craig, Michelle, Robert, and Douglas Taylor, who each offered unique perspectives, along with Ashley Taylor, who researched details, located photographs, and shared meaningful stories about her grandmother. Several members of the Taylors' house staff graciously provided assistance, including Josie, Maggie, and especially Dores, the long-time caretaker of Taylor's wardrobe, who was especially helpful in putting together the ensembles.

An exhibition and catalogue of this magnitude cannot be realized without the contributions of many individuals and organizations. My most sincere gratitude goes to our sponsors and supporters: U.S. Trust, Barbara Anderson Stoiber, The Ruth and Vernon Taylor Foundation, The Virginia M. Ullman Foundation, as well as Arizona Costume Institute, Barbara and Craig Barrett, Jacquie Dorrance, The Bruce T. Halle Family Foundation, Ellen Katz, Sharron Lewis, Miriam and Yefim Sukhman, and additionally Susan Drescher-Mulzet and Gay Wray.

Many figures in the fashion world deserve my warm thanks and respect. I am deeply appreciative of Hubert de Givenchy for his elegant and insightful remarks, which speak to the great importance of Taylor's collection. Marie-Andrée Jouve kindly provided valuable information on Balenciaga's pieces. Homer Layne ensured the accurate description of Charles James's garments. Thanks also go to Tatiana Sorokko, Ralph Rucci, and Glenda Bailey, as well as Fern Mallis, Harriet Weintraub, and Stuart Cohen.

I am indebted to photographer Ken Howie, who went far beyond the call of duty to capture the clothes at their very best. I also thank Theresa Howie for her enduring support, and Dane Nordine, John Colonna, Shawn Arney, and Jeff Tully for their specialized knowledge of color, printing, and scanning. I am appreciative beyond measure of the catalogue's editor, Elizabeth Stepina Zinn. The book's elegant design was skillfully handled by Chaves Design, and I am most grateful for their collaborative nature and respect for the garments. David Boatman deserves recognition for capturing the spirit of Taylor in the short film he produced to accompany the exhibition. Special thanks go to the many family friends who granted our request for interviews, including Walter and Mary Curley, Robin Chandler Duke, Elizabeth Fondaras, Count Ferdinand von Galen, Sheika Gramshammer, Harriett Kelly, Thomas Kempner, Jr., Nancy Kissinger, Kenneth Jay Lane, Dina Merrill, Katherine "Kitty" Ockenden, Patsy Preston, Stan Rumbaugh, Gay Wray, and Lynn Wyatt. Their insights greatly enhanced the catalogue, exhibition, and video.

At Phoenix Art Museum, I am extremely grateful to James K. Ballinger, Sybil Harrington Director, for his unwavering support. Curatorial Assistant Helen Nosova deserves special recognition for her work on all aspects of the project. Thanks also go to our dedicated interns, Casey Hagarty and Deborah Missel. Marketing and public relations were deftly handled by Mindi Carr and Arian Ploszaj. Kristi McMillan created inspiring programs in conjunction with the exhibition. Registration and shipping of the objects were adeptly coordinated by Leesha Alston and Alexis Gould. David Restad, with the aid of preparators Gene Koeneman, Bob Gates, and Zack Glover, was responsible for the smart installation design. Lee Werhan and the staff of the Museum's store also deserve thanks for constantly advising, bolstering, and championing the project.

Last and most importantly, I would like to reiterate my gratitude to the Taylor family. It has been truly an honor and inspiration to work with them on the presentation of this outstanding collection.

Dennita Sewell
CURATOR OF FASHION DESIGN